ADAM GILCHRIST COLOUR

AUSTRALIAN CRICKETER

MR VIVEK KUMAR PANDEY SHAMBHUNATH

ISBN 979-888555203-5

Short biography of Adam Gilchrist and about life.During writing this book no character & no religious are harmed written by Mr Vivek Kumar Pandey. winner youngest writer award 1st rank in india 2020.He is only one writer can publish 760+ own book that was greatest successfull in his life.This All Credit Goes To My Super Hero Daddy. This book fully colour Edition.

Contents

Foreword

Author biography in English :MY NAME IS VIVEK KUMAR PANDEY . I WAS BORN IN 30 SEP 2002,I AM FROM SURAT GUJARAT INDIA.MY DREAM WAS TO BE GOOD WRITERS ,MY FAMILY SUPPORTED ME TO SUCCESSFUL AND I CAN DO IT MY SELF.How do I write? That is a question, I believe, that can be honestly answered by me."CELEBRATING YOUNGEST WRITER AWARD WINNER IN GUJARAT 1ST RANK" MR PANDEY JI . I may think I did a good job writing something . The reader is the one who decides the quality of my writing. I do find writing to be natural to me and therefore find it to be a real challenge. My trick as a challenged writer is to do the best I can and know that I am happy with the final outcome. It may take a while to do my best and there may be quite a few problems I run into along the way.

I am not a greedy person those who are thinking about me and my self I never tried it anyone people suffering from sadness ,I trying to get promoted people suffering from happiness and joy in your Life Time. Now in current situation in India and also world people are unemployed and have no many but our indian governor help to people to get free food from ration card , i also take part in leadership team ,i am Motivational speaker , Film script writer. There was my two dream firstly writer and secondly actor & also my own film is upcoming soon i done almost completely completed script for my film .I AM GOING TO SAY WORD OF HEART TOUCH OUT PLEASE READ IT" , firstly i thanks my father he supports me in this field they always getting inspired me by own his words and behavior ,they always said that he was a biggest person in the world in future and also they purchase fruit and chocolate for me in anytime & anyway , firstly my father buy him then call me Vivek you want a chocolate i will say yes papa but how many tell me ,papa: you tell me how much i buy him i told 1 or 2 chocolate but my father purchase whole the boxes of chocolate and they get suprised me. MY FATHER WAS BORN IN " 20 SEPTEMBER" 1971 IN INDIA.

1) MY FATHER FAVORITE CLOTHES IS KURTA PAIJMA AND ALSO STYLES SHOE

2) FAVORITE SINGER IS KISHORE DA

3) FAVORITE STATE GUJARAT AND KOLKATA , HIS VILLAGE IN BIHAR

4) FAVORITE COLOR BLACK AND WHITE

THEY ALSO LOVE cricket like IPL and one day t-20 .they also like watching a News daily and heard the song daily ,they also interested in tik tok video but in current time tik tok is banned in india but also few videos are in you tube. In lockdown time my family and me very enjoy day daily. my father play daily ludo with his sister and son, daughter.they always loved tea and coffee anytime call me "। ववकि थोडा़ चाय बनाओना ववकि तुम्हारे हाथ का चाय अच्छा लगता है". I make it tea for my father but some reason after the April to june they are suffering from fever and cough , weakness on 6 June 2020 my father death. they not told me say bye bye his life. After death of 6 June on 10 june my mom and dad anniversary.but my father is Best in the world they can do anything for me please take care of father and respect it of your parents.

Preface

Mr Vivek Kumar Pandey Also Written Bollywood Hit Film & Backstage Writer Of Film Golmaal Again,Bhuj,Laxmii

CHAPTER ONE

Adam Gilchrist Colour

- Adam Gilchrist

1. Disclaimer : During writing this book no character & no religious are harmed written by Mr Vivek Kumar Pandey.

Adam Craig Gilchrist AM born 14 November 1971 is an Australian cricket commentator and former international cricketer and captain of the Australia national cricket team. He was an attacking left-handed batsman and record-breaking wicket-keeper, who redefined the role for the Australia national team through his aggressive batting. Widely regarded as one of the greatest wicket-keeper-batsman in the history of the game, Gilchrist held the world record for the most dismissals by a wicket-keeper in One Day International (ODI) cricket until it was surpassed by Kumar Sangakkara in 2015 and the most by an Australian in Test cricket.

His strike rate is amongst the highest in the history of both ODI and Test cricket; his 57 ball century against England at Perth in December 2006 is the fourth-fastest century in all Test cricket. He was the first player to have hit 100 sixes in Test cricket. His 17 Test centuries and 16 in ODIs are both second only to Sangakkara by a wicket-keeper. He holds the unique record of scoring at least 50 runs in successive World Cup finals (in 1999, 2003 and 2007). His 149 off 104 balls against Sri Lanka in the 2007 World Cup final is rated one of the greatest World Cup innings of all time. He is one of the only three players to have won three World Cup titles.

Gilchrist was renowned for walking when he considered himself to be out, sometimes contrary to the decision of the umpire. He made his first-class debut in 1992, his first One-Day International appearance in 1996 in India and his Test debut in 1999. During his career, he played for Australia in 96 Test matches and over 270 One-day internationals. He was Australia's regular vice-captain in both forms of the game, captaining the team when regular captains Steve Waugh and Ricky Ponting were unavailable. He retired from international cricket in March 2008, though he continued to play domestic tournaments until 2013.

- personal life

Adam Gilchrist was born in 1971 at Bellingen Hospital, in Bellingen, New South Wales, the youngest of four children. He and his family lived in Dorrigo, Junee and then Deniliquin where, playing for his school, Deniliquin South Public School, he won the Brian Taber Shield (named after New South Wales cricketer Brian Taber). When Adam was 13, his parents, Stan and June, moved the family to Lismore where he captained the Kadina High School cricket team. Gilchrist was selected for the state under-17 team, and in 1989 he was offered a scholarship by London-based Richmond Cricket Club, a scheme he now supports himself. During his year at Richmond, he also played junior cricket for Old Actonians Cricket Club's under-17 team, with whom he won the Middlesex League and Cup double. He moved to Sydney and joined the Gordon District Cricket Club in Sydney Grade Cricket, later moving to Northern Districts.

Gilchrist is married to his high school sweetheart Melinda (Mel) Gilchrist (née Sharpe), a dietitian, and they have three sons and a daughter. His family came under the spotlight in the months leading up to the 2007 Cricket World Cup as one impending birth threatened his presence in the squad; the child was born in February and Gilchrist was able to take part in the tournament.

- Domestic career

In 1991, Gilchrist was selected for the Australia Young Cricketers, a national youth team that toured England and played in youth ODIs and Tests. Gilchrist scored a century and a fifty in the three Tests. Upon his return to Australia late in the year, Gilchrist was accepted into the Australian Cricket Academy. Over the next year, Gilchrist represented the ACA as they played matches against the Second XI of Australia's state teams, and toured South Africa to play provincial youth teams.

Upon returning to Australia, Gilchrist scored two centuries in four matches for the state Colts and Second XI teams, and was rewarded with selection to make his first-class debut for New South Wales during the 1992–93 season, although he played purely as a batsman, due to the presence of incumbent wicketkeeper Phil Emery. In his first season, the side won the Sheffield Shield, Gilchrist scoring an unbeaten 20 in the second innings to secure an easy win over Queensland in the final. Gilchrist made 274 runs at an average of 30.44 in his debut season, a score of 75 being his only effort beyond fifty. He also made his debut in Mercantile Mutual limited overs competition. He struggled to keep his place in the side, playing only three first-class matches in the following season. He scored on 43 runs at 8.60; New South Wales won both competitions, but Gilchrist was overlooked for both finals and did not play a single limited overs match.

Due to a lack of opportunities in the dominant New South Wales outfit, Gilchrist joined Western Australia at the start of the 1994–95, where he had to compete with former Test player Tim Zoehrer for the wicket-keeper's berth. Gilchrist had no guarantee of selection. However, he made a century in a pre-season trial match and seized Zoehrer's place. The local fans were initially hostile to the move, but Gilchrist won them over.

He made 55 first-class dismissals in his first scason, thc most by any wicketkeeper in Australian domestic cricket in 1994–95. However, he struggled with the bat, scoring 398 runs at 26.53 with seven single figure scores, although he recorded his maiden first-class century in the latter stages of the season, with 126 against South Australia. Gilchrist was rewarded with selection in the Young Australia team that toured England in 1995 and played matches against the English counties. Gilchrist starred with bat, scoring 490 runs at 70.00 with two centuries.

His second season based in Perth saw him top of the dismissals again, with 58 catches and four stumpings, but, significantly, 835 runs at an impressive batting average of 50.52. The Warriors made it to the final of the Sheffield Shield, at the Adelaide Oval, where Gilchrist scored 189 not out in the first innings, from only 187 balls, including five sixes.The innings brought Gilchrist national prominence. The match ended in a thrilling draw as South Australia's last-wicket pair held on to fend off the visitors. The hosts thus took the title, having scored more points in the qualifying matches.

Gilchrist also scored an unbeaten 76 to help Western Australia secure a narrow three-wicket victory over New South Wales in the penultimate limited overs match of the season, which saw them into the final against Queensland, which was lost. Gilchrist's form saw him selected for Australia A, a team comprising players close to national selection.

At the start of the 1996–97 season, sections of the media advocated that he replace Ian Healy as the national wicket-keeper, but Healy struck 161 in the First Test and maintained his position. Gilchrist continued to perform strongly on the domestic circuit he topped the dismissals count once again, with 62, along with a batting average of just under 40, although he failed to post a century. Team success came in the Mercantile Mutual Cup, where the Warriors won by eight wickets against Queensland in the March 1997 final; Gilchrist was not required to bat.

The 1997–98 season ended with Gilchrist top of the dismissals chart for the fourth season in a row with an improved batting average of 47.66, despite playing in only six of the ten qualifying Shield matches due to his becoming a regular member of the national limited overs team. Gilchrist registered his maiden–first-class double century with an unbeaten 203 against South Australia early in the season, before returning late in the season after his international commitments were over. He added 109 against Victoria, and played in the Sheffield Shield final victory over Tasmania, although he scored only eight. There was disappointment for the team in the Mercantile Mutual Cup, losing the semi-final to Queensland.The following season saw Gilchrist's domestic appearances diminish due to his international commitments: he made only a single appearance in the Mercantile Mutual Cup,but still managed to help Western Australia defend the Sheffield Shield, scoring a century in the qualifying rounds.

Gilchrist's regular selection for Australia meant that he was rarely available for domestic selection after he became the Test wicket-keeper in late-1999 between 1999 and 2005, he made only seven first-class appearances for his state. He did not play in the 2005–06 Pura Cup and only appeared three times in the limited-overs ING Cup.

- Indian Premier League

Gilchrist played a total of six seasons in the Indian Premier League (IPL), the major Twenty20 franchise league in India, three for Deccan Chargers and three for Kings XI Punjab. He was signed by Deccan for the 2008 season, the inaugural season of the competition, having been purchased for US$700,000 in the player auction a few months after his retirement from international cricket.

Before the fourth season of the IPL Gilchrist was bought at the 2011 player auction by Kings XI Punjab for US$900,000 and was, again, appointed as captain, taking over from Kumar Sangakkara who had moved to Deccan. In March 2012 he was named player-coach of the side for the following season, replacing his friend and former Australia teammate Michael Bevan, whose contract as head coach was not renewed. After the team failed to make the play-offs, Gilchrist speculated that he may choose to retire from cricket.

Following the appointment of Darren Lehmann, who had previously worked with Gilchrist at Deccan, as head coach, Gilchrist chose to play one more IPL season for Kings XI, once again as captain. In May 2013, Gilchrist announced his retirement from the IPL. A planned appearance in the first season of the Caribbean Premier League had to be cancelled after an ankle injury and the match proved to be Gilchrist's last in top-class cricket. In that fixture, Gilchrist took the wicket of Harbhajan Singh, from his one and only ball he ever bowled in a T20 match.

Over his six seasons in the IPL Gilchrist played a total of 82 matches, 48 for Deccan and 34 for Kings XI. He scored more than 2,000 runs, including two centuries. He was also the first cricketer to score 1000 runs in IPL.

Gilchrist signed a short-term contract in November 2009 to play Twenty20 cricket for Middlesex County Cricket Club in England during 2010. He was appointed interim captain of the T20 side on 11 June following the sudden resignation of Shaun Udal. He played in seven matches for the side during the 2010 Twenty20 Cup, scoring 212 runs at an average of 30.28, including a century made against Kent at Canterbury, as well as captaining the county against the touring Australians in a one-day match ahead of their ODI series against England.The season was Gilchrist's only one spent playing county cricket.

- International career

Celebrating a century against the World XI in the second ICC Super Series match at Telstra Dome (7 October 2005).

Gilchrist was called up for the Australian One Day International (ODI) team in 1996, his debut coming against South Africa at Faridabad on 25 October 1996 as the 129th Australian ODI cap, after an injury to incumbent Ian Healy. While not particularly impressive with the bat on his debut, scoring 18 before being bowled by Allan Donald, Gilchrist took his first catch as an international wicketkeeper, Hansie Cronje departing for a golden duck from the bowling of Paul Reiffel.

He was run out for a duck in his only other ODI on the tour. Healy resumed his place during the 1996–97 season. Gilchrist replaced Healy for the first two ODIs in the 1997 Australian tour of South Africa, after Healy was suspended for dissent. When Healy returned Gilchrist maintained his position in the team as a specialist batsman after Mark Waugh sustained a hand injury. It was during this series that Gilchrist made his first ODI half-century, with an innings of 77 in Durban. He totalled 127 runs at 31.75 for the series. Gilchrist went on to play in the Texaco Trophy later in 1997 in the 3–0 series loss against England, scoring 53 and 33 in two innings.

At the start of the 1997–98 Australian season, Healy and captain Mark Taylor were omitted from the ODI squad as the Australian selectors opted for Gilchrist and Michael di Venuto. Gilchrist's elevation was made possible by a change in policy by selectors, who announced that selection for ODI and Test teams would be separate, with Test and ODI specialists selected accordingly, while Healy remained the preferred Test wicket-keeper.

This came after Australia failed to qualify for the previous season's ODI triangular series final for the first time in 17 years. The new team was initially unconvincing, losing all four round robin matches against South Africa in the 1997–98 Carlton & United Series, with multiple players filling Taylor's role as Mark Waugh's opening partner without success. Gilchrist also struggled batting in the lower order at number seven, the conventional wicket-keeper's batting position, scoring 148 runs at 24.66 in the eight qualifying matches. In the first final against South Africa at the Melbourne Cricket Ground Gilchrist was selected as Waugh's opening partner. In a particularly poor start to the new combination, Waugh was run out after a mix-up with Gilchrist. However, in the second final, Gilchrist struck his maiden ODI century, spearheading Australia's successful run chase at the Sydney Cricket Ground, securing his position as an opening batsman. Australia won the third final to claim the title.

Touring New Zealand in February 1998, Gilchrist topped the Australia averages with 200 runs at 50.00, including a match-winning 118 in the first match. He also effected his first ODI stumping, the wicket of Nathan Astle in the Second ODI in Wellington. Australia then played two triangular tournaments in Asia. Gilchrist struggled in India, scoring 86 runs at 17.20. He went on to play in the Coca-Cola Cup in Sharjah in April 1998, a triangular tournament between Australia, India and New Zealand. Australia finished runners-up in the tournament, with Gilchrist taking nine dismissals as wicketkeeper and averaging 37.13 with the bat.

Gilchrist won a silver medal at the 1998 Commonwealth Games in Kuala Lumpur, the only time cricket has been in the Commonwealth Games. The matches did not have ODI status, and after winning their first four fixtures, Australia lost the final to South Africa, Gilchrist making 15.[He then scored 103 and ended with 190 runs at 63.33 as Australia took a rare 3–0 whitewash on Pakistani soil.

Gilchrist was in fine form ahead of the 1999 Cricket World Cup with a productive individual performance in the Carlton & United Series in January and February 1999 against Sri Lanka and England. He finished with 525 runs at a batting average of 43.75 with two centuries—both against Sri Lanka—and a fifty, and a total of 27 dismissals in 12 matches. His 131 helped Australia set a successful run-chase at the SCG, and he followed this with 154 at the MCG. The 1999 tour of the West Indies was Australia's last campaign before the World Cup and continued to prove Gilchrist's ability as a wicketkeeper-batsman. Gilchrist, with a batting average of 28.71 and a strike rate of nearly 90.00, and seven fielding dismissals in a seven-match series which ended 3–3 with one tie.

- First World Cup success : 1999 Cricket World Cup

Gilchrist played in every match of Australia's successful World Cup campaign, but struggled at first, with scores of 6, 14 and 0 in the first three matches against Scotland, New Zealand and Pakistan. Australia lost the latter two matches and had to avoid defeat for six consecutive matches to reach the final. Gilchrist's quick-fire 63 runs in 39 balls against Bangladesh helped the Australians into the Super Six stage of the tournament, which was secured with a win over the West Indies, although Gilchrist made only 21. Gilchrist continued to struggle in the Super Six phase, scoring 31, 10 and 5 against India, Zimbabwe and South Africa. Australia won all three matches, the last in the final over,to scrape into the semifinals. Gilchrist made only 20 in the semifinal against South Africa, but completed the final act of the match. With the scores tied, South Africa were going for the winning run when Gilchrist broke the stumps to complete the run out of Allan Donald the match was tied, and Australia proceeded to the final as they had won the group stage match against South Africa. Gilchrist's 54 in the final helped secure Australia's first world title since 1987 with an eight wicket victory over Pakistan. It was a happy ending for Gilchrist, who had struggled through the tournament, with 237 runs at 21.54.

Success at the World Cup was followed by a defeat by Sri Lanka in the final of the Aiwa Cup in August 1999, Gilchrist was the most successful batsman and wicket-keeper of the tournament, with 231 runs at 46.20. While the Test players battled against Sri Lanka, Gilchrist led Australia A in a limited overs series against India A in Los Angeles. He then scored 60 runs at 20.00 as the Australians completed a 3–0 whitewash of Zimbabwe in October.

- Test debut

Gilchrist made his Test match debut in the First Test against Pakistan at the Gabba in Brisbane in November 1999 becoming the 381st Australian Test cricketer. He replaced Healy, who was dropped after a run of poor form, despite the incumbent's entreaties to the selectors to allow him a farewell game in front of his home crowd. Gilchrist's entry into the Test arena coincided with a dramatic rise in Australia's fortunes. Up to this point, they had played eight Tests in 1999, winning and losing three.

Gilchrist's icy reception at the Gabba did not faze him he took five catches, stumped Azhar Mahmood off Shane Warne's bowling and scored a rapid 81, mostly in partnership with ODI partner Waugh, in a match that Australia won comfortably by ten wickets. In his second Test match he made an unbeaten 149 to help guide Australia to victory in a game that looked well beyond their reach. Australia were struggling at 5/126 in pursuit of 369 for victory as he joined his Western Australian teammate, Justin Langer, but the pair put on a record-breaking partnership of 238 to seal an Australian win. Gilchrist continued his strong run throughout his debut Test season, and ended the summer with 485 runs at 69.28 in six matches, three each against Pakistan and India, adding two fifties against the latter.

Gilchrist was moderately successful in the following ODIs, the Carlton & United Series; Australia defeated Pakistan 2–0 in a best-of-three final. Gilchrist scored 272 runs at 27.20; his best effort was 92 in a 152-run victory over India on Australia Day. Gilchrist then scored 251 runs at 41.66 in the ODIs during a tour of New Zealand. The highlight was a 128 in Christchurch that propelled Australia to a score of 6/349. Gilchrist was named man of the match in two of the games.

In the Third Test against New Zealand in 2000, Gilchrist recorded the third best Test performance ever by a wicketkeeper, and the best by an Australian, taking ten catches in the match. Although Gilchrist's batting was modest, yielding 144 runs at 36.00, Australia took a 3–0 clean sweep. In two home and away ODI series against South Africa, Gilchrist had a quiet time, scoring 170 runs at 26.66. South Africa won three of the six matches, with one tie.

The 2000–01 season saw a West Indian touring party and Gilchrist warmed up with consecutive first-class centuries for Western Australia. Captaining his Test team for the first time in place of the injured Steve Waugh in the Third Test in Adelaide. Gilchrist scored only 9 and 10 not out, but a ten-wicket haul from Colin Miller resulted in a hard-fought five-wicket victory for Australia. Gilchrist described the match as "the proudest moment of my career".Waugh resumed the captaincy on his return to the team for the Fourth and Fifth Tests, with the series finishing in a 5–0 whitewash. Gilchrist scored 241 runs at 48.20 with two fifties. In the ensuing ODI tournament, Gilchrist scored 326 runs at 36.22 with a top-score of 98 as the Australians won all ten matches.

Up to this point, Gilchrist had played in 14 Tests, all in Australasia, and all of which had been won. Australia's run of 15 consecutive Test wins faced a steep challenge on the tour of India, where they had not won a Test series since 1969–70.

Australia's streak looked in danger during the First Test in Mumbai when they fell to 5/99 in reply to India's 171 when Gilchrist came to the crease. He counterattacked savagely, scoring 122 in just 112 balls, and featuring in a 197-run partnership with Matthew Hayden in only 32 overs. This swung the momentum back to Australia, who reached 349. Gilchrist took six catches and was named Man of the Match in a ten wicket victory, extending the world record run to 16.

Gilchrist's form dipped momentarily, with a rare king pair (two golden ducks in the same match) in the Second Test in Kolkata and just two runs in his two innings in Chennai. He was out LBW four consecutive times in the last two Tests, three of these to Harbhajan Singh, who took 32 wickets in the series to end Australia's run by inflicting a 2–1 series loss. His one-day form remained strong, with 172 runs at 43.00 in the ODI series in India, as Australia bounced back to win the series 3–2. During this series he captained the ODI team for the first time, winning all three of the matches under his captaincy.

- Ashes 2001

Gilchrist played a pivotal role in the 2001 Ashes series which Australia won 4–1, with 340 runs at a batting average of 68.00 and 26 dismissals in the five match series.

Gilchrist warmed up by putting his ODI struggles on English soil in 1999 behind him, scoring 248 runs at 49.60 in the triangular tournament preceding the Tests, scoring an unbeaten 76 in the final win over Pakistan.

- Gilchrist put the disappointment of India behind him in the First Test at Edgbaston, scoring 152 from only 143 balls. The allowed Australia to reach 576 in only 545 minutes, and set up an innings victory that set the tone for the series. Gilchrist then added 90 in the eight-wicket win in the Second Test at Lord's, before turning the tide in the Third Test at Trent Bridge. Australia slumped to 7/105 in reply to the hosts' 185, but Gilchrist's 54 took the tourists to 190 before a seven-wicket win resulted in the retention of the Ashes.

Gilchrist captained the team in the Fourth Test at Headingley after an injury to Steve Waugh.After persistent rain interruptions, Gilchrist declared with Australia four down at tea on the fourth day, leaving England with a target of 315, which, despite losing two early wickets, they reached with six wickets to spare, (Mark Butcher scoring an unbeaten 173, including 24 boundaries). Gilchrist failed to pass 25 in the last two Tests, but it had been a productive season; he scored centuries in both of Australia's county matches.

- Two home series followed in the 2001–02 season, a fully drawn (0–0) three match series against New Zealand and a whitewash over South Africa 3–0. Gilchrist scored 118 in the First Test against New Zealand and an unbeaten 83 in the Third Test in Perth as the Australians held on for a draw with three wickets intact. However, Gilchrist did little in the triumph over South Africa, failing to pass 35. He ended the summer Tests with 353 runs at 50.42.

In the ensuing ODIs, Gilchrist scored only 97 runs at 16.16.The Australian selectors sought to accommodate Hayden, who had been successful as a Test opener, into the ODI team by rotating him with Gilchrist and Waugh, but this appeared to unsettle the team. With a newly fragile top-order, Australia failed to qualify for the finals, and the Waugh brothers were dropped from the team, ending Gilchrist's four-year partnership with Mark. Ricky Ponting was promoted to the captaincy ahead of vice captain Gilchrist.

- The Australians then toured South Africa the next month and it was during the First Test in Johannesburg that Gilchrist broke the record for the fastest double century in Tests on 23 February, requiring 212 balls for the feat. This was eight balls quicker than Ian Botham's innings against India at The Oval in 1982. He ended unbeaten on 204, having featured in a partnership of 317 with Damien Martyn at a run rate of 5.5. South Africa were demoralised and lost by an innings after being forced to follow on. The record lasted only one month, however, with New Zealand's Nathan Astle taking 59 balls less to reach the milestone during an innings in March 2002.

In the Second Test at Cape Town, Gilchrist struck 138 from 108 balls to set up a first innings lead and eventual four-wicket win. He then top-scored with 91 in the Third Test, and although Australia lost the match, Gilchrist ended the series with an astonishing 473 at 157.66 from just 474 balls, in addition to 14 dismissals.

Gilchrist captained the ODI team, once again for a single match, against Kenya in Nairobi during the PSO Tri-Nation Tournament. Despite Australia's unbeaten run in the competition, the final, against Pakistan was abandoned due to rain, so the teams shared the trophy. During the six middle months of 2002, Gilchrist played in 18 ODIs, scoring 562 runs at 31.22, including a century, recovering from his slump.

After scoring 122 runs at 40.66 in the 3–0 Test series clean sweep over Pakistan in the United Arab Emirates, Gilchrist went on to help the Australians retain The Ashes 4–1 in 2002–03, playing in all five matches of the series, finishing with 330 runs at 55.50 and taking 25 dismissals as wicket-keeper. After scoring fifties in the first two Tests, Gilchrist scored a counter-attacking 133 from 121 balls in the Fifth Test at the SCG, but was unable to prevent Australia's only loss of the series.

From the time of his debut up to the 2003 World Cup, Gilchrist's played in 40 Tests in series.With the exception of the 2001 tour of India, when he averaged 24.80 (he made 124 runs in the series; 122 of them came in one innings), his performances with the bat were such that he was described at the time as the "finest batsman-wicketkeeper to have graced the game". At one point in March 2002, Gilchrist's Test average was over 60; the second-highest for any established player in Test history, and he topped the ICC Test batting rankings in May 2002.

Gilchrist warmed up for the World Cup in South Africa by scoring 310 runs at 44.28 in the triangular tournament in Australia against England and Sri Lanka. His performances over the past year were recognised with the Allan Border Medal.

- 2003 Cricket World Cup

Gilchrist played in all but one of the matches in Australia's successful defence of their World Cup title; he was rested for the group match against the Netherlands. He finished the tournament with 408 runs at an average of 40.80 at a strike rate of 105. He scored four half-centuries, and was run out against Sri Lanka in the Super Six stage just a single run short of a century.

In the semi-final, he scored 22 before being caught off an inside-edge onto pad off the bowling of Aravinda de Silva. The umpire gave no reaction, however Gilchrist walked off the pitch after a moment's pause. In 2009 it was described as an "astonishing moment" drawing criticism from England's Angus Fraser, who "objected to him being canonised simply for not cheating", and from others who "thought that he walked almost by accident; that having played his shot he overbalanced in the direction of the pavilion." His actions nevertheless drew praise from the majority.In the final, India elected to field first and Gilchrist hammered 57 from 48 balls, featuring in a century opening stand with Hayden to seize the initiative. This laid the foundation for Australia's 2/359 and a crushing 125-run win, ending an unbeaten campaign. Gilchrist was also the competition's most successful wicketkeeper, making 21 dismissals.

Success in the World Cup was followed up by a tour of the West Indies where Gilchrist was part of a side that won both the ODI and Test series. He scored 282 runs at 70.50 with one century in the four Tests, and 212 runs at 35.33 in the ODIs. The Australians then defeated a touring Bangladeshi cricket team in short series in both forms of the game. Gilchrist was only sporadically required with the bat.

- Decline and revival

After scoring his first Test century at his home ground in Perth, an unbeaten 113 against Zimbabwe, Gilchrist's Test form dipped again during the 2003–04 season, with only 120 runs coming in the next 10 innings, during the home series against India (drawn 1–1) and the away series in Sri Lanka (won 3–0). However, he returned to form in the Second Test Kandy, scoring a quickfire 144 in the second innings to set up a 27-run win after Australia conceded a 91-run first innings lead.

However, he maintained high standards in ODIs during this period, including 111 against India in Bangalore, 172 against Zimbabwe, just one run short of Mark Waugh's Australian record, and two further half-centuries in the VB Series in Australia. His success in One-day cricket was underlined by his rise to the top of the ICC ODI batting rankings in February 2004. However, he was unable to maintain this form on the 2004 tours of Sri Lanka, Zimbabwe and the Champions Trophy in England, accumulating 253 runs at 28.11 in 11 innings.

Gilchrist then scored 115 runs at 28.75 in two Tests at home to Sri Lanka in mid-2004, and captained in the First Test win in Darwin with Ponting absent. Australia won the series 1–0.

A 104 in the First Test against India in October 2004 proved to be a false renaissance he scored only 104 runs in the remaining seven innings on the Indian tour and 139 runs in eight ODI innings towards the end of the 2004–05 season, which formed the lowest average period of Gilchrist's career until 2007. He took the captaincy of the Test team once again, in place of the injured Ricky Ponting,and led the Australian side to a historic 2–1 series victory in India, a feat last achieved in 1969.Ponting recovered to lead the team in the Fourth Test, Australia's only loss.

Gilchrist returned to form when New Zealand toured Australia at the start of southern hemisphere season. He scored 126 and 50 in the 2–0 Test series clean sweep and scored fifties in both ODIs. He then scored 230 runs at 76.66 in three Tests against Pakistan, including a rapid 113 in the Third Test at the SCG as Australia won all five Tests during the summer. He made it three successive Test centuries with 121 and 162 in the first two Tests on the tour of New Zealand, before ending with an unbeaten 60 in the Third Test; he totalled 343 runs at 114.33 for the series. His ODI form in the early part of 2005 remained moderate, with 308 runs at 28.00 during the southern summer.December 2005. At his home ground, the WACA, Gilchrist faces Makhaya Ntini, in the First Test, Australia v South Africa.

Gilchrist was in strong form ahead of the Tests, scoring 393 runs at 49.13 in the ODIs in England. The highlight was the 121 not out in the final game of the one-day NatWest Series, Gilchrist being awarded the man-of-the-match award. However, he performed poorly in the five Tests, with 204 runs at 25.50. Just as in India in 2001, Australia lost 2–1.

Australia and Gilchrist returned to form after the Ashes in the series against the ICC World XI. Gilchrist scored 45, 103 and 32 as Australia swept the ODIs 3–0, and top-scored with 94 in the first innings of the one-off Test, which Australia won. However, this did not transfer into the regular international matches. In six home Tests against the West Indies and South Africa in 2005–06, Gilchrist managed only 190 runs at 23.75, but Australia was unhindered, winning 3–0 and 2–0 respectively.

- Gilchrist with Australia in 2006

His one-day form also began to suffer, scoring only 11 runs in three ODIs in New Zealand and 13 in the first two matches of the VB Series. He was rested for two games and returned to form against Sri Lanka on 29 January 2006 on his home ground, the WACA, hitting 116 runs off 105 balls to lead Australia to victory. He continued in this vein with the fastest ever century by an Australian in just 67 balls against Sri Lanka at the Gabba, ending with 122 as Australia won the deciding third final by nine wickets. After a slow start, he ended the series with 432 runs at 48.00.

The purple patch ended on the tour of South Africa and then Bangladesh. He scored 206 runs at 29.42 in five Tests and 248 runs at 35.42 in eight ODIs, inflated by a 144 in the First Test against Bangladesh. Despite this, Australia won all five Tests. Gilchrist scored 130 runs at 26.00, including a 92 against the West Indies as Australia won the 2006 Champions Trophy in India.

- On 16 December 2006, during the Third Ashes Test at the WACA, Gilchrist scored a century in 57 balls, including twelve fours and four sixes, which at the time was the second fastest recorded Test century. At 97 runs from 54 balls, Gilchrist needed three runs from the next delivery to better Viv Richards' record set in 1986. The ball delivered by

Matthew Hoggard was wide and Gilchrist was unable to score from it. He later claimed that the "batting pyrotechnics" had been the result of a miscommunication between Michael Clarke and him with the Australian captain Ricky Ponting; Gilchrist had actually been told not to score quick runs with a view to declaring the innings.

He ended the 2006–07 Ashes with a century and two fifties, totalling 229 runs at 45.80 at a strike rate of over 100 as Australia regained the Ashes with a 5–0 whitewash. It was an inconsistent series; aside from three scores mentioned, Gilchrist failed to pass one in his other three innings. Between Ashes series, Gilchrist had averaged only 25 with one Test century.

However, both he and Australia suffered a surprising string of poor results in the 2006–07 Commonwealth Bank Series, Gilchrist managing an average of only 22.20 during the tournament. Australia won seven of their eight qualifying matches, but England won with two finals victories over the Australians. Gilchrist scored 60 and 61 in the first two matches but did not pass 30 thereafter. He was then rested for Australia's winless three-match ODI tour of New Zealand, before his selection for the 2007 Cricket World Cup. Having previously indicated that it was highly likely that he would retire after the 2007 World Cup, he then stated a desire to play on afterwards.

- 2007 Cricket World Cup

Gilchrist and Australia started their 2007 World Cup campaign by winning all three of their matches in Group A, against Scotland, the Netherlands and South Africa. Australia won all six of their matches in the Super8 stage with little difficulty—the margins of victory exceeded 80 runs or six wickets in every instance. They topped the table and thus qualifying for a semi-final rematch against fourth-placed South Africa. Gilchrist opened the Australian batting in each match, taking a pinch-hitting role in the opening powerplays. Initially successful in the group matches, scoring 46, 57 and 42, he failed in the first Super8 match against West Indies (7), but bounced back to score a second half-century (59 not out) in a ten-wicket victory against Bangladesh in a match drastically shortened due to rain. After a run of middling scores, he failed again in the final Super8 match against New Zealand.

As a batsman, Gilchrist was dismissed for a single run in the semi-final against South Africa, despite which Australia won by seven wickets. Gilchrist opened the batting against Sri Lanka in the final. This was Gilchrist's third successive World Cup final, and the third time he scored at least 50 runs in a World Cup final and he went on to make his only ever century in a world cup match (his previous best World Cup score having been 99 against Sri Lanka in the 2003 tournament). Gilchrist went on to score 149 runs off 104 balls with thirteen fours and eight sixes, the highest individual score in a World Cup final, eclipsing his captain Ricky Ponting's score of 140 in the 2003 final. Australia won and he was named the man of the match. Subsequently there has been some controversy over Gilchrist's use of a squash ball inside his glove during this innings. The MCC stated that Gilchrist had not acted against the laws or the spirit of the game, since there is no restriction against the external or internal form of batting gloves.

- Gilchrist batting at the MCG vs India

In September 2007, Gilchrist played in the inaugural World Twenty20. He scored 169 runs at 33.80 as Australia were knocked out by India in the semifinals. Gilchrist then scored 208 runs at 34.66 as Australia took an away ODI series against India 4–2. In November, Gilchrist's peers voted him the greatest Australian ODI cricketer ever, for which he was awarded an honour at an ACA function before Australia's second Test against Sri Lanka.He was only required to bat once in the Tests, and made 67 not out as Australia swept Sri Lanka aside 2–0.

- Retirement

On 26 January 2008 during the 4th and final Test of the 2007–08 series against India, Gilchrist announced that he would retire from international cricket at the end of the season. A back injury kept Ricky Ponting off the field for sections of the Indian's second innings, resulting in Gilchrist captaining the team for part of the final two days of his Test cricket career. India batted out the match for a draw, so Gilchrist's 14 in the first innings was his final Test innings; he took his 379th and final catch when Virender Sehwag was caught behind. Gilchrist had scored only 150 runs at 21.42 in his final Test series.

John Buchanan, who coached Australia during most of Gilchrist's international career, predicted that Gilchrist's retirement would have more impact than the previous year's retirements of Damien Martyn, Glenn McGrath, Shane Warne and Justin Langer and Australian Prime Minister Kevin Rudd asked Gilchrist to reconsider. Gilchrist later revealed that he chose to retire after dropping VVS Laxman during the first innings, and realising that he had lost his "competitive edge." He played out the summer's ODI series, before ending in disappointment when India beat Australia 2–0 in the 2007–08 Commonwealth Bank Series finals.Gilchrist managed only seven and two in the finals. His highlight of the series was his scoring 118 and being named Man of the Match in his final match at his adopted home in Perth on 15 February 2008, against Sri Lanka. He ended his final series with 322 runs at 32.20.

- Playing style

Gilchrist standing up to Shane Warne in 2005. Andrew Strauss is the batsman.

Gilchrist's attacking batting was a key part of Australia's one-day success, as he usually opened the batting. He was a part of the successful 1999, 2003 and 2007 Cricket World Cup campaigns. Gilchrist's Test batting average in the upper 40s is unusually high for a wicket-keeper.

He retired from Test cricket at 45th on the all–time list of highest batting averages. At the end of his Test career he had established a Test strike-rate of 82 runs per hundred balls, at the time the third highest since balls were recorded in full. His combination of attack and consistency create one of the most dynamic world cricketers ever, playing shots to all areas of the field with uncommon timing. He was second on the all-time list of most sixes in Tests at 100 with only Brendon McCullum ahead of him with 107.

Gilchrist's skills as a wicket-keeper were sometimes questioned; some claimed that he was the best keeper in Australia whilst others that Victorian wicket-keeper Darren Berry was the best Australian wicket-keeper of the 1990s and early 2000s. Gilchrist attributed his batting techniques from early training with his father, where he would defend shots, sometimes only gripping the bat with his top (right) hand, and would end a session to simply play attacking shots with tennis balls to end on a positive and fun note. He also adopted a naturally high grip where both hands were closer to the end of the handle for more top hand control.

Gilchrist successfully kept wicket for fast bowlers Glenn McGrath and Brett Lee for most of his international career. His partnerships with McGrath and Lee are second and fourth respectively in both test and ODI history for the number of wickets taken.With Alec Stewart and Mark Boucher, he shares the record for most catches (6) by a wicketkeeper in a ODI match, having achieved this feat five times. In 2007 he took six dismissals and scored a half century in the same ODI for the second time; he remains the only player to do so even once. At Old Trafford in August 2005, he passed Alec Stewart's world record of 4,540 runs as a Test wicketkeeper,and at his retirement in 2008, he was the most successful ODI wicket-keeper with 472 dismissals (417 catches and 55 stumpings), more than 80 dismissals ahead of his closest rival, Mark Boucher. This record was surpassed seven years later by Kumar Sangakkara.

- Walking and discipline

It is unusual for professional batsmen to "walk"; that is, to agree that they have been dismissed and leave the field of play without waiting for (or contrary to) an umpire's decision. Gilchrist reignited this debate by walking during a high-profile match, the 2003 World Cup semi-final against Sri Lanka, after the umpire ruled him to be not out. He has since proclaimed himself to be "a walker", or a batsman who will consistently walk, and has done so on numerous occasions. On one occasion against Bangladesh, Gilchrist walked but TV replays failed to suggest any contact between his bat and the ball. Without such contact, he could not have been caught out.

Gilchrist's actions have sparked debate amongst current and former players and umpires. Ricky Ponting has declared on several occasions that he is not a walker but will leave it to each player to decide whether they wish to walk or not. While no other Australian top order batsmen have expressly declared themselves to be walkers, lower-order batsmen Jason Gillespie and Michael Kasprowicz both walked during Test matches in India in 2004. In 2004, New Zealand captain Stephen Fleming accused Gilchrist of conducting a "walking crusade" when Craig McMillan refused to walk after Gilchrist had caught him off an edge from the bowling of Jason Gillespie in the First Test in Brisbane.

After the appeal was turned down by the umpire, who did not hear the edge, Gilchrist goaded McMillan about the edge, and McMillan's angry response was picked up by the stump microphone: "...not everyone is walking, Gilly ... not everyone has to walk, mate...". The taunt was effective, however, as McMillan, perhaps distracted, missed the next ball and was given out leg before wicket. Gilchrist said in his autobiography that he had "zero support in the team" for his stance and that he felt that the topic made the dressing room uncomfortable. He added that he "felt isolated" and "silently accused of betraying the team. Implicitly I was made to feel selfish, as if I was walking for the sake of my own clean image, thereby making everyone else look dishonest."

Gilchrist has been noted for his emotional outbursts on the cricket field, and has been fined multiple times for dissent against umpiring decisions. In January 2006, he was fined 40% of his match fee in an ODI against South Africa. In another instance, in early 2004 in Sri Lanka, Gilchrist audibly argued with umpire Peter Manuel after batting partner Andrew Symonds was given out. After the argument concluded, Manuel consulted umpiring partner Billy Bowden and reversed his decision, recalling Symonds to the crease. Gilchrist was also reprimanded by the Australian Cricket Board for publicly questioning the legality of Muttiah Muralitharan's bowling action in 2002, as his comments were found to be in breach of the clause in the player code of conduct relating to "detrimental public comment".

During the 2003 World Cup, Gilchrist accused Pakistani wicketkeeper Rashid Latif of making a racist remark towards him while the latter was batting in their group match. Latif who was cleared by match referee Clive Lloyd, threatened to sue Gilchrist for this claim.

- Achievements & Awards

Gilchrist was one of five Wisden Cricketers of the Year for 2002, and Australia's One-day International Player of the Year in 2003 and 2004. He was awarded the Allan Border Medal in 2003, and was the only Australian cricketer who was a current player at the time to have been named in "Richie Benaud's Greatest XI" in 2004. He was selected in the ICC World XI for the charity series against the ACC Asian XI, 2004–05, was voted as "World's Scariest Batsman" in a poll of international bowlers, and was named as wicket-keeper and opening batsman in Australia's "greatest ever ODI team."

In a poll of over ten thousand people hosted in 2007 by ESPNcricinfo, he was voted the ninth greatest all-rounder of the last one hundred years. A panel of prominent cricket writers selected him in Australia's all-time best XI for ESPNcricinfo. Gilchrist has not only left his mark on Australian cricket but the whole cricketing world. In 2010, Gilchrist was made a Member of the Order of Australia (AM) for his services to cricket and the community. He was inducted into the Sport Australia Hall of Fame in 2012. On 9-December-2013, ICC announced that they had inducted Gilchrist in the prestigious ICC Hall of Fame.He was named an Australia Post Legend of Cricket in 2021.

CHAPTER TWO

Australia national cricket team

- Australia national cricket team

The Australia men's national cricket team represents Australia in men's international cricket. As the joint oldest team in Test cricket history, playing in the first ever Test match in 1877, the team also plays One-Day International (ODI) and Twenty20 International (T20I) cricket, participating in both the first ODI, against England in the 1970–71 season and the first T20I, against New Zealand in the 2004–05 season, winning both games. The team draws its players from teams playing in the Australian domestic competitions – the Sheffield Shield, the Australian domestic limited-overs cricket tournament and the Big Bash League.

The national team has played 837 Test matches, winning 397, losing 226, drawing 212 and tying 2. As of January 2021, Australia is ranked third in the ICC Test Championship on 113 rating points. Australia is the most successful team in Test cricket history, in terms of overall wins, win-loss ratio and wins percentage.

Test rivalries include The Ashes (with England), The Border-Gavaskar Trophy (with India), the Frank Worrell Trophy (with the West Indies), the Trans-Tasman Trophy (with New Zealand), and with South Africa.

The team has played 958 ODI matches, winning 581, losing 334, tying 9 and with 34 ending in a no-result. As of January 2021, Australia is ranked fourth in the ICC ODI Championship on 111 rating points, though have been ranked first for 141 of 185 months since its introduction in 2002.

Australia is the most successful team in ODI cricket history, winning more than 60 per cent of their matches, with a record seven World Cup final appearances (1975, 1987, 1996, 1999, 2003, 2007 and 2015) and have won the World Cup a record five times: 1987, 1999, 2003, 2007 and 2015. Australia is the first (and only) team to appear in four consecutive World Cup finals (1996, 1999, 2003 and 2007), surpassing the old record of three consecutive World Cup appearances by the West Indies (1975, 1979 and 1983) and the first and only team to win 3 consecutive World Cups (1999, 2003 and 2007). The team was undefeated in 34 consecutive World Cup matches until the 2011 Cricket World Cup where Pakistan beat them by 4 wickets in the Group stage.

It is also the second team to win a World Cup (2015) on home soil, after India (2011). Australia have also won the ICC Champions Trophy twice (2006 and 2009) making them the first and the only team to become back to back winners in the Champions Trophy tournaments. As of 2021, Australia is the only team to win five Cricket World Cups; no other team has won more than two.

The national team has played 153 Twenty20 International matches, winning 79, losing 69, tying 2 and with 3 ending in a no-result. As of November 2021, Australia is ranked sixth in the ICC T20I Championship on 246 rating points. Australia are the reigning ICC Men's T20 World Cup champions, defeating New Zealand in the 2021 final to claim their first T20 World Cup title.

On 12 January 2019, Australia won the first ODI against India at the Sydney Cricket Ground by 34 runs, to record their 1,000th win in international cricket.

- Australian cricket from 1876–77 to 1890

The Australian team that toured England in 1878

The Australian cricket team participated in the first Test match at the MCG in 1877, defeating an English team by 45 runs, with Charles Bannerman making the first Test century, a score of 165 retired hurt.Test cricket, which only occurred between Australia and England at the time, was limited by the long distance between the two countries, which would take several months by sea. Despite Australia's much smaller population, the team was very competitive in early games, producing stars such as Jack Blackham, Billy Murdoch, Fred "The Demon" Spofforth, George Bonnor, Percy McDonnell, George Giffen and Charles "The Terror" Turner. Most cricketers at the time were either from New South Wales or Victoria, with the notable exception of George Giffen, the star South Australian all-rounder.

A highlight of Australia's early history was the 1882 Test match against England at The Oval. In this match, Fred Spofforth took 7/44 in the game's fourth innings to save the match by preventing England from making their 85-run target. After this match The Sporting Times, a major newspaper in London at the time, printed a mock obituary in which the death of English cricket was proclaimed and the announcement made that "the body was cremated and the ashes taken to Australia." This was the start of the famous Ashes series in which Australia and England play a series of Test matches to decide the holder of the Ashes. To this day, the contest is one of the fiercest rivalries in sport.

- Golden age

History of Australian cricket from 1890–91 to 1900 and History of Australian cricket from 1900–01 to 1918

The so-called 'Golden Age' of Australian Test cricket occurred around the end of the 19th century and the beginning of the 20th century, with the team under the captaincy of Joc Darling, Monty Noble and Clem Hill winning eight of ten tours. It is considered to have lasted from the 1897–98 English tour of Australia and the 1910–11 South African tour of Australia. Outstanding batsmen such as Joe Darling, Clem Hill, Reggie Duff, Syd Gregory, Warren Bardsley and Victor Trumper, brilliant all-rounders including Monty Noble, George Giffen, Harry Trott and Warwick Armstrong and excellent bowlers including Ernie Jones, Hugh Trumble, Tibby Cotter, Bill Howell, Jack Saunders and Bill Whitty, all helped Australia to become the dominant cricketing nation for most of this period.

Victor Trumper became one of Australia's first sporting heroes, and was widely considered Australia's greatest batsman before Bradman and one of the most popular players. He played a record (at the time) number of Tests at 49 and scored 3163 (another record) runs at a high for the time average of 39.04. His early death in 1915 at the age of 37 from kidney disease caused national mourning. The Wisden Cricketers' Almanack, in its obituary for him, called him Australia's greatest batsman: "Of all the great Australian batsmen Victor Trumper was by general consent the best and most brilliant."

The years leading up to the start of World War I were marred by conflict between the players, led by Clem Hill, Victor Trumper and Frank Laver, the Australian Board of Control for International Cricket, led by Peter McAlister, who was attempting to gain more control of tours from the players. This led to six leading players (the so-called "Big Six") walking out on the 1912 Triangular Tournament in England, with Australia fielding what was generally considered a second-rate side. This was the last series before the war, and no more cricket was played by Australia for eight years, with Tibby Cotter being killed in Palestine during the war.

- Australian cricket from 1918–19 to 1930

Test cricket resumed in the 1920/21 season in Australia with a touring English team, captained by Johnny Douglas losing all five Tests to Australia, captained by the "Big Ship" Warwick Armstrong. Several players from before the war, including Warwick Armstrong, Charlie Macartney, Charles Kelleway, Warren Bardsley and the wicket-keeper Sammy Carter, were instrumental in the team's success, as well as new players Herbie Collins, Jack Ryder, Bert Oldfield, the spinner Arthur Mailey and the so-called "twin destroyers" Jack Gregory and Ted McDonald. The team continued its success on the 1921 tour of England, winning three out of the five Tests in Warwick Armstrong's last series. The side was, on the whole, inconsistent in the latter half of the 1920s, losing its first home Ashes series since the 1911–12 season in 1928–29.

- Australian cricket from 1930–31 to 1945

The 1930 tour of England heralded a new age of success for the Australian team. The team, led by Bill Woodfull – the "Great Un-bowlable" – featured legends of the game including Bill Ponsford, Stan McCabe, Clarrie Grimmett and the young pair of Archie Jackson and Don Bradman. Bradman was the outstanding batsman of the series, scoring a record 974 runs, including one century, two double centuries and one triple century, a massive score of 334 at Leeds which including 309 runs in a day. Jackson died of tuberculosis at the age of 23 three years later, after playing eight Tests. The team was widely considered unstoppable, winning nine of its next ten Tests.

The 1932–33 England tour of Australia is considered one of the most infamous episodes of cricket, due to the England team's use of bodyline, where captain Douglas Jardine instructed his bowlers Bill Voce and Harold Larwood to bowl fast, short-pitched deliveries aimed at the bodies of the Australian batsmen. The tactic, although effective, was widely considered by Australian crowds as vicious and unsporting. Injuries to Bill Woodfull, who was struck over the heart, and Bert Oldfield, who received a fractured skull (although from a non-bodyline ball), exacerbated the situation, almost causing a full-scale riot from the 50 000 fans at the Adelaide Oval for the third Test.

The conflict almost escalated into a diplomatic incident between the two countries, as leading Australian political figures, including the Governor of South Australia, Alexander Hore-Ruthven, protested to their English counterparts. The series ended in a 4–1 win for England but the bodyline tactics used were banned the year after.

The Australian team put the result of this series behind them, winning their next tour of England in 1934. The team was led by Bill Woodfull on his final tour and was notably dominated by Ponsford and Bradman, who twice put on partnerships of over 380 runs, with Bradman once again scoring a triple-century at Leeds. The bowling was dominated by the spin pair of Bill O'Reilly and Clarrie Grimmett, who took 53 wickets between them, with O'Reilly twice taking seven-wicket hauls.

Sir Donald Bradman is widely considered the greatest batsman of all time. He dominated the sport from 1930 until his retirement in 1948, setting new records for the highest score in a Test innings (334 vs England at Headingley in 1930), the most runs (6996), the most centuries (29), the most double centuries and the highest Test and first-class batting averages. His record for the highest Test batting average – 99.94 – has never been beaten. It is almost 40 runs per innings above the next highest average. He would have finished with an average of over 100 runs per innings if he had not been dismissed for a duck in his last Test. He was knighted in 1949 for services to cricket. He is generally considered one of Australia's greatest sporting heroes.

Test cricket was again interrupted by war, with the last Test series in 1938 made notable by Len Hutton scoring a world record 364 for England, with Chuck Fleetwood-Smith conceding 298 runs in England's world record total of 7/903. Ross Gregory, a notable young batsman who played two Tests before the war, was killed in the war.

- Australian cricket from 1945–46 to 1960

The team continued its success after the end of the Second World War, with the first Test (also Australia's first against New Zealand) being played in the 1945–46 season against New Zealand. Australia was by far the most successful team of the 1940s, being undefeated throughout the decade, winning two Ashes series against England and its first Test series against India. The team capitalised on its ageing stars Bradman, Sid Barnes, Bill Brown and Lindsay Hassett while new talent, including Ian Johnson, Don Tallon, Arthur Morris, Neil Harvey, Bill Johnston and the fast bowling pair of Ray Lindwall and Keith Miller, who all made their debut in the latter half of the 1940s, and were to form the basis of the team for a good part of the next decade. The team that Don Bradman led to England in 1948 gained the moniker The Invincibles, after going through the tour without losing a single game.

Of 31 first-class games played during the tour, they won 23 and drew 8, including winning the five-match Test series 4–0, with one draw. The tour was particularly notable for the fourth Test of the series, in which Australia won by seven wickets chasing a target of 404, setting a new record for the highest run chase in Test cricket, with Arthur Morris and Bradman both scoring centuries, as well as for the final Test in the series, Bradman's last, where he finished with a duck in his last innings after needing only four runs to secure a career average of 100.

Australia was less successful in the 1950s, losing three consecutive Ashes series to England, including a horrendous 1956 Tour of England, where the 'spin twins' Laker and Lock destroyed Australia, taking 61 wickets between them, including Laker taking 19 wickets in the game (a first-class record) at Headingley, a game dubbed Laker's Match.

However, the team rebounded to win five consecutive series in the latter half of the 1950s, first under the leadership of Ian Johnson, then Ian Craig and Richie Benaud. The series against the West Indies in the 1960–61 season was notable for the Tied Test in the first game at the Gabba, which was the first in Test cricket. Australia ended up winning the series 2–1 after a hard-fought series that was praised for its excellent standards and sense of fair play. Stand-out players in that series as well as through the early part of the 1960s were Richie Benaud, who took a then-record number of wickets as a leg-spinner and who also captained Australia in 28 Tests, including 24 without defeat; Alan Davidson, who was a notable fast-bowler and also became the first player to take 10 wickets and make 100 runs in the same game in the first Test; Bob Simpson, who also later captained Australia for two different periods of time; Colin McDonald, the first-choice opening batsman for most of the 1950s and early '60s; Norm O'Neill, who made 181 in the Tied Test; Neil Harvey, towards the end of his long career; and Wally Grout, an excellent wicket-keeper who died at the age of 41.

- World Series Cricket and Restructuring

The Centenary Test was played in March 1977 at the MCG to celebrate 100 years since the first Test was played. Australia won the match by 45 runs, an identical result to the first Test match.

In May 1977, Kerry Packer announced he was organising a breakaway competition – World Series Cricket (WSC) – after the Australian Cricket Board (ACB) refused to accept Channel Nine's bid to gain exclusive television rights to Australia's Test matches in 1976. Packer secretly signed leading international cricketers to his competition, including 28 Australians. Almost all of the Australian Test team at the time were signed to WSC – notable exceptions including Gary Cosier, Geoff Dymock, Kim Hughes and Craig Serjeant and the Australian selectors were forced to pick what was generally considered a third-rate team from players in the Sheffield Shield. Former player Bob Simpson, who had retired 10 years previously after a conflict with the board, was recalled at the age of 41 to captain Australia against India. Jeff Thomson was named deputy in a team that included seven debutants. Australia managed to win the series 3–2, mainly thanks to the batting of Simpson, who scored 539 runs, including two centuries; and the bowling of Wayne Clark, who took 28 wickets.

Australia lost the next series 3–1 against the West Indies, which was fielding a full strength team; and also lost the 1978–79 Ashes series 5–1, the team's worst Ashes result in Australia. Graham Yallop was named as captain for the Ashes, with Kim Hughes taking over for the 1979–80 tour of India. Rodney Hogg took 41 wickets in his debut series, an Australian record. WSC players returned to the team for the 1979–80 season after a settlement between the ACB and Kerry Packer. Greg Chappell was reinstated as captain.

The underarm bowling incident of 1981 occurred when, in an ODI against New Zealand, Greg Chappell instructed his brother Trevor to bowl an underarm delivery to New Zealand batsman Brian McKechnie, with New

Zealand needing a six to tie off the last ball. The aftermath of the incident soured political relations between Australia and New Zealand, with several leading political and cricketing figures calling it "unsportsmanlike" and "not in the spirit of cricket".

Australia continued its success up until the early 1980s, built around the Chappell brothers, Dennis Lillee, Jeff Thomson and Rod Marsh. The 1980s was a period of relative mediocrity after the turmoil caused by the Rebel Tours of South Africa and the subsequent retirement of several key players. The rebel tours were funded by the South African Cricket Board to compete against its national side, which had been banned—along with many other sports, including Olympic athletes—from competing internationally, due to the South African government's racist apartheid policies. Some of Australia's best players were poached: Graham Yallop, Carl Rackemann, Terry Alderman, Rodney Hogg, Kim Hughes, John Dyson, Greg Shipperd, Steve Rixon and Steve Smith amongst others. These players were handed three-year suspensions by the Australian Cricket Board which greatly weakened the player pool for the national sides, as most were either current representative players or on the verge of gaining honours.

- Australian cricket from 1985–86 to 2000

The so-called 'Golden Era' of Australian cricket occurred around the end of the 20th century and the beginning of the 21st century. This was a period in which Australian cricket recovered from the disruption caused by World Series Cricket to create arguably the strongest Test team in history.

Under the captaincy of Allan Border and the new fielding standards put in place by new coach Bob Simpson, the team was restructured and gradually rebuilt their cricketing stocks. Some of the rebel players returned to the national side after serving their suspensions, including Trevor Hohns, Carl Rackemann and Terry Alderman. During these lean years, it was the batsmen Border, David Boon, Dean Jones, the young Steve Waugh and the bowling feats of Alderman, Bruce Reid, Craig McDermott, Merv Hughes and to a lesser extent, Geoff Lawson who kept the Australian side afloat.

With the emergence of players such as Ian Healy, Mark Taylor, Geoff Marsh, Mark Waugh, and Greg Matthews in the late 1980s, Australia was on the way back from the doldrums. Winning the Ashes in 1989, the Australians got a roll on beating Pakistan, Sri Lanka and then followed it up with another Ashes win on home soil in 1991. The Australians went on to the West Indies and had their chances but ended up losing the series. However, they bounced back and beat the Indians in their next Test series. With the retirement of the champion but defensive, Allan Border, a new era of attacking cricket had begun under the leadership of firstly Mark Taylor and then Steve Waugh.

The 1990s and early 21st century were arguably Australia's most successful periods, unbeaten in all Ashes series played bar the famous 2005 series and achieving a hat-trick of World Cups. This success has been attributed to the restructuring of the team and system by Border, successive aggressive captains, and the effectiveness of several key players, most notably Glenn McGrath, Shane Warne, Justin Langer, Matthew Hayden, Steve Waugh, Adam Gilchrist, Michael Hussey and Ricky Ponting.

- Australian cricket from 2000–01

Following the 2006–07 Ashes series which Australia won 5 nil, Australia slipped in the rankings after the retirements of key players. In the 2013/14 Ashes series, Australia again defeated England 5 nil and climbed back to third in the ICC International Test rankings. In February/March 2014, Australia beat South Africa, the number 1 team in the world, 2–1 and overtook them to return to the top of the rankings. In 2015, Australia won the World Cup, losing just one game for the tournament.

As of December 2020, Australia are ranked first in the ICC Test Championship, fourth in the ICC ODI Championship and second in the ICC T20I Championship.

- 2018 Australian ball-tampering scandal

On 25 March 2018, during the third Test match against hosts South Africa; players Cameron Bancroft, Steve Smith, David Warner and the leadership group of the team were implicated in a ball tampering scandal. Smith and Bancroft admitted to conspiring to alter the condition of the ball by rubbing it with a piece of adhesive tape containing abrasive granules picked up from the ground (it was later revealed that sandpaper was used). Smith stated that the purpose was to gain an advantage by unlawfully changing the ball's surface in order to generate reverse swing.

Bancroft had been filmed tampering with the ball and after being informed he had been caught, he was seen to transfer a yellow object from a pocket to the inside front of his trousers to hide the evidence. Steve Smith and David Warner were stood down as captain and vice-captain during the third Test while head coach, Darren Lehmann was suspected to have assisted Cameron Bancroft to tamper the ball.

The ICC imposed a one-match ban and 100%-match-fee fine on Smith, while Bancroft was fined 75 per cent of his match fee and received 3 demerit points. Smith and Warner were both stripped of their captaincy roles by Cricket Australia and sent home from the tour (along with Bancroft). Tim Paine was appointed as captain for the fourth Test. Cricket Australia then suspended Smith and Warner from playing for 12 months and Bancroft for 9 months. Smith and Bancroft could not be considered for leadership roles for 12 months after the suspension, while Warner is banned from leadership of any Cricket Australia team for life.

In the aftermath of these events, Darren Lehmann announced his resignation as head coach at the end of the series with Justin Langer replacing him. On 8 May 2018, Tim Paine was also named as the ODI captain while Aaron Finch was reinstated as T20I captain hours later, although Finch replaced Paine as the ODI captain after the 5-0 ODI series whitewash in England in June 2018.

On 7 October 2018, Australia played their first Test match under new coach Justin Langer and a new leadership group, which included Tim Paine as Australia's 46th Test captain. After a 1–0 loss to Pakistan in a two match Test series against Pakistan in the UAE and a 2–1 defeat against India in a four match Test series, they found success against Sri Lanka, winning the two Test match series 2–0.

In 2019, Australia played in the Cricket World Cup, where they finished second in the group stage before being knocked out by England at Edgbaston in the semi-final. Australia went on to retain the Ashes during the 2019 Ashes series, the first time on English soil since 2001, by winning the fourth Test at Old Trafford.

In 2020–21, Australia hosted India for 3 ODIs, 3 T20Is, and 4 Tests. They won the ODI series 2–1, but lost the T20I series 2–1. Then, the two teams competed for the Border-Gavaskar Trophy which saw one of the greatest overseas Test triumphs by India in the 4th Test to win the series 2–1 with the 3rd Test being drawn.

- Team colours

For Test matches, the team wears Cricket Whites, with an optional sweater or sweater-vest with a green and gold V-neck for use in cold weather. The sponsor's (currently Alinta for home matches and Qantas for away matches) logo is displayed on the right side of the chest while the Cricket Australia emblem is displayed on the left. If the sweater is being worn the Cricket Australia emblem is displayed under the V-neck and the sponsor's logo is again displayed on the right side of the chest. The baggy green, the Australian Test cricket cap, is considered an essential part of the cricketing uniform and as a symbol of the national team, with new players being presented with one upon their selection in the team. The cap and the helmet both prominently display the Australian cricketing coat-of-arms instead of the Cricket Australia emblem. At the end of 2011, ASICS was named the manufacturer of the whites and limited over uniforms from Adidas, with the ASICS logo being displayed on the shirt and pants. Players may choose any manufacturer for their other gear (bat, pads, shoes, gloves, etc.).

In One Day International (ODI) cricket and Twenty20 International cricket, the team wears uniforms usually coloured green and gold, the national colours of Australia. There has been a variety of different styles and layouts used in both forms of the limited-overs game, with coloured clothing (sometimes known as "pyjamas") being introduced for World Series Cricket in the late 1970s. The Alinta or Qantas logo is prominently displayed on the shirts and other gears. The current home ODI kit consists of green as the primary colour and gold as the secondary colour. The away kit is the opposite of the home kit with gold as the primary colour and green as the secondary colour. The home Twenty20 kit consists of black with the natural colours of Australia, green and gold strips. However, since Australia beat New Zealand at the MCG in the 2015 Cricket World Cup wearing the gold uniform, it has also become their primary colour, with the hats used being called 'floppy gold', formerly known as 'baggy gold', a limited-overs equivalent to a baggy green. Until the early 2000s and briefly in early 2020, in ODIs, Australia wore yellow helmets, before using green helmets as in test matches.

Former suppliers were Asics (1999), ISC (2000–2001), Fila (2002–2003) and Adidas (2004–2010) among others. Before Travelex, some of the former sponsors were Coca-Cola (1993–1998), Fly Emirates (1999) and Carlton & United Breweries (2000–2001).

- match records
- Team

1. Australia is the most successful Test team in cricketing history. It has won more than 350 Test matches at a rate of almost 47%. The next best performance is by South Africa at 37%.
2. Australia have been involved in the only two Tied Tests played. The first occurred in December 1960, against the West Indies in Brisbane.The second occurred in September 1986, against India in Madras (Chennai).
3. Australia's largest victory in a Test match came on 24 February 2002. Australia defeated South Africa by an innings and 360 runs in Johannesburg.
4. Australia holds the record for the most consecutive wins with 16. This has been achieved twice; from October 1999 to February 2001 and from December 2005 to January 2008.
5. Australia shares the record for the most consecutive series victories winning 9 series from October 2005 to June 2008. This record is shared with England.
6. Australia's highest total in a Test match innings was recorded in Kingston, Jamaica against the West Indies in June 1955. Australia posted 758/8 in their first innings, with five players scoring a century.
7. Australia's lowest total in a Test match innings was recorded in Birmingham against England in May 1902. Australia were bowled all out for 36.
8. Australia are the only team to have lost a Test match after enforcing the follow-on, having been the losing side in all three such matches
9. The first Test in the 1894–95 Ashes.
10. The third Test of the 1981 Ashes.
11. The second Test in the 2000–01 Border-Gavaskar Trophy series against India.
12. Against India in March 2013, Australia became the first team in Test history to declare in their first innings and then lose by an innings.
13. In the 2013–14 Ashes series, Australia took all 100 wickets on offer in the 5–0 sweep over England.
14. Ricky Ponting and Steve Waugh have played in the most Test matches for Australia, both playing in 168 matches.

- Batting

1. Charles Bannerman faced the first ball in Test cricket, scored the first runs in Test cricket and also scored the first Test century.
2. Charles Bannerman also scored 67.34% of the Australian first innings total in match 1. This record remains to this day as the highest percentage of a completed innings total that has been scored by a single batsman.
3. Ricky Ponting has scored the most runs for Australia in Test cricket with 13,378 runs. Allan Border is second with 11,174 runs in 265 innings a record which was broken by Brian Lara during his innings of 226 against Australia while Steve Waugh has 10,927 in 260 innings.Allan Border was the first Australian batsman to pass 10,000 and the first ever batsman to pass 11,000 Test runs.Ricky Ponting was the first Australian batsman to pass 12,000 and 13,000 Test runs.
4. Matthew Hayden holds the record for the most runs in a single innings by an Australian with 380 in the first Test against Zimbabwe in Perth in October 2003.
5. Donald Bradman holds the record for the highest average by an Australian (or any other) cricketer of 99.94 runs per dismissal. Bradman played 52 Tests, scoring 29 centuries and a further 13 fifties.
6. Ricky Ponting holds the record for the most centuries by an Australian cricketer with 41. Former Australian captain Steve Waugh is in second position with 32 centuries from 260 innings.
7. Allan Border holds the record for the most fifties by an Australian cricketer with 63 in 265 innings.
8. Adam Gilchrist holds the record for the fastest century by an Australian.
9. Glenn McGrath holds the record for the most ducks by an Australian cricketer with 35 in 138 innings.

- Bowling

1. Billy Midwinter picked up the first five-wicket haul in a Test innings in match 1.
2. Fred Spofforth performed Test cricket's first hat-trick by dismissing Vernon Royle, Francis McKinnon and Tom Emmett in successive balls.
3. Fred Spofforth also took the first 10-wicket match haul in Test cricket.

4. Shane Warne holds the record for the most wickets by an Australian cricketer with 708 wickets in 145 Test matches.
5. Arthur Mailey holds the record for the best bowling figures in an innings by an Australian cricketer with 9/121 against England in February 1921.
6. Bob Massie holds the record for the best bowling figures in a match by an Australian cricketer with 16/137 against England in June 1972. That was also his first Test match for Australia.
7. J. J. Ferris holds the record for the best bowling average by an Australian bowler, taking 61 wickets at 12.70 in his career.
8. Clarrie Grimmett holds the record for the most wickets in a Test series with 44 against South Africa in 1935–36.

- Fielding and wicketkeeping

1. Ricky Ponting holds the record for the most catches in a career by an Australian fielder with 196 in 168 matches.
2. Jack Blackham performed the first stumping in Test cricket in match 1.
3. Adam Gilchrist holds the record for the most dismissals in a career by an Australian wicketkeeper with 416 in 96 matches.

- Team

1. Australia's highest total in a One-Day International innings is 434/4, scored off 50 overs against South Africa in Johannesburg on 12 March 2006. This was a world record score before the South Africans later surpassed it in the same match.
2. Australia's lowest total in a One-Day International innings is 70. This score has occurred twice; once against England in 1977 and once against New Zealand in 1986.
3. Australia's largest victory in One-Day International cricket is 275 runs. This occurred against Afghanistan at the 2015 World Cup in Australia.
4. Australia are the only team in the history of the World Cup to win 3 consecutive tournaments; 1999, 2003 and 2007.
5. Australia went undefeated at the World Cup for a record 34 consecutive matches. After being defeated by Pakistan in 1999, Australia would remain unbeaten until they were again defeated by Pakistan in 2011.
6. Australia have won the most World Cups – 5.

CHAPTER THREE

Let's Know About Cricket

- Cricket

Cricket is a bat-and-ball game played between two teams of eleven players on a field at the centre of which is a 22-yard (20-metre) pitch with a wicket at each end, each comprising two bails balanced on three stumps. The game proceeds when a player on the fielding team, called the bowler, "bowls" (propels) the ball from one end of the pitch towards the wicket at the other end. The batting side's players score runs by striking the bowled ball with a bat and running between the wickets, while the bowling side tries to prevent this by keeping the ball within the field and getting it to either wicket, and dismiss each batter (so they are "out"). Means of dismissal include being bowled, when the ball hits the stumps and dislodges the bails, and by the fielding side either catching a hit ball before it touches the ground, or hitting a wicket with the ball before a batter can cross the crease line in front of the wicket to complete a run. When ten batters have been dismissed, the innings ends and the teams swap roles. The game is adjudicated by two umpires, aided by a third umpire and match referee in international matches.

Forms of cricket range from Twenty20, with each team batting for a single innings of 20 overs and the game generally lasting three hours, to Test matches played over five days. Traditionally cricketers play in all-white kit, but in limited overs cricket they wear club or team colours. In addition to the basic kit, some players wear protective gear to prevent injury caused by the ball, which is a hard, solid spheroid made of compressed leather with a slightly raised sewn seam enclosing a cork core layered with tightly wound string.

The earliest reference to cricket is in South East England in the mid-16th century. It spread globally with the expansion of the British Empire, with the first international matches in the second half of the 19th century. The game's governing body is the International Cricket Council (ICC), which has over 100 members, twelve of which are full members who play Test matches. The game's rules, the Laws of Cricket, are maintained by Marylebone Cricket Club (MCC) in London. The sport is followed primarily in South Asia, Australasia, the United Kingdom, southern Africa and the West Indies.Women's cricket, which is organised and played separately, has also achieved international standard. The most successful side playing international cricket is Australia, which has won seven One Day International trophies, including five World Cups, more than any other country and has been the top-rated Test side more than any other country.

- History of cricket to 1725

A medieval "club ball" game involving an underhand bowl towards a batter. Ball catchers are shown positioning themselves to catch a ball. Detail from the Canticles of Holy Mary, 13th century.

Cricket is one of many games in the "club ball" sphere that basically involve hitting a ball with a hand-held implement; others include baseball (which shares many similarities with cricket, both belonging in the more specific bat-and-ball games category), golf, hockey, tennis, squash, badminton and table tennis. In cricket's case, a key difference is the existence of a solid target structure, the wicket (originally, it is thought, a "wicket gate" through which sheep were herded), that the batter must defend. The cricket historian Harry Altham identified three "groups" of "club ball" games: the "hockey group", in which the ball is driven to and fro between two targets (the goals); the "golf group", in which the ball is driven towards an undefended target (the hole); and the "cricket group", in which "the ball is aimed at a mark (the wicket) and driven away from it".

It is generally believed that cricket originated as a children's game in the south-eastern counties of England, sometime during the medieval period.Although there are claims for prior dates, the earliest definite reference to cricket being played comes from evidence given at a court case in Guildford in January 1597 (Old Style), equating to January 1598 in the modern calendar. The case concerned ownership of a certain plot of land and the court heard the testimony of a 59-year-old coroner, John Derrick, who gave witness that.

Being a scholler in the ffree schoole of Guldeford hee and diverse of his fellows did runne and play there at creckett and other plaies.

Given Derrick's age, it was about half a century earlier when he was at school and so it is certain that cricket was being played c. 1550 by boys in Surrey. The view that it was originally a children's game is reinforced by Randle Cotgrave's 1611 English-French dictionary in which he defined the noun "crosse" as "the crooked staff wherewith boys play at cricket" and the verb form "crosser" as "to play at cricket".

One possible source for the sport's name is the Old English word "cryce" (or "cricc") meaning a crutch or staff. In Samuel Johnson's Dictionary, he derived cricket from "cryce, Saxon, a stick". In Old French, the word "criquet" seems to have meant a kind of club or stick. Given the strong medieval trade connections between south-east England and the County of Flanders when the latter belonged to the Duchy of Burgundy, the name may have been derived from the Middle Dutch (in use in Flanders at the time) "krick"(-e), meaning a stick (crook). Another possible source is the Middle Dutch word "krickstoel", meaning a long low stool used for kneeling in church and which resembled the long low wicket with two stumps used in early cricket. According to Heiner Gillmeister, a European language expert of Bonn University, "cricket" derives from the Middle Dutch phrase for hockey, met de (krik ket)sen (i.e., "with the stick chase"). Gillmeister has suggested that not only the name but also the sport itself may be of Flemish origin.

- Growth of amateur and professional cricket in England

Evolution of the cricket bat. The original "hockey stick" (left) evolved into the straight bat from c. 1760 when pitched delivery bowling began.

Although the main object of the game has always been to score the most runs, the early form of cricket differed from the modern game in certain key technical aspects; the North American variant of cricket known as wicket retained many of these aspects. The ball was bowled underarm by the bowler and along the ground towards a batter armed with a bat that in shape resembled a hockey stick; the batter defended a low, two-stump wicket; and runs were called notches because the scorers recorded them by notching tally sticks.

In 1611, the year Cotgrave's dictionary was published, ecclesiastical court records at Sidlesham in Sussex state that two parishioners, Bartholomew Wyatt and Richard Latter, failed to attend church on Easter Sunday because they were playing cricket. They were fined 12d each and ordered to do penance.This is the earliest mention of adult participation in cricket and it was around the same time that the earliest known organised inter-parish or village match was played – at Chevening, Kent. In 1624, a player called Jasper Vinall died after he was accidentally struck on the head during a match between two parish teams in Sussex.

Cricket remained a low-key local pursuit for much of the 17th century. It is known, through numerous references found in the records of ecclesiastical court cases, to have been proscribed at times by the Puritans before and during the Commonwealth. The problem was nearly always the issue of Sunday play as the Puritans considered cricket to be "profane" if played on the Sabbath, especially if large crowds or gambling were involved.

According to the social historian Derek Birley, there was a "great upsurge of sport after the Restoration" in 1660. Gambling on sport became a problem significant enough for Parliament to pass the 1664 Gambling Act, limiting stakes to £100 which was, in any case, a colossal sum exceeding the annual income of 99% of the population. Along with prizefighting, horse racing and blood sports, cricket was perceived to be a gambling sport.Rich patrons made matches for high stakes, forming teams in which they engaged the first professional players.By the end of the century, cricket had developed into a major sport that was spreading throughout England and was already being taken abroad by English mariners and colonisers – the earliest reference to cricket overseas is dated 1676. A 1697 newspaper report survives of "a great cricket match" played in Sussex "for fifty guineas apiece" – this is the earliest known contest that is generally considered a First Class match.

- The patrons, and other players from the social class known as the "gentry", began to classify themselves as "amateurs" to establish a clear distinction from the professionals, who were invariably members of the working class, even to the point of having separate changing and dining facilities. The gentry, including such high-ranking nobles as the Dukes of Richmond, exerted their honour code of noblesse oblige to claim rights of leadership in any sporting contests they took part in, especially as it was necessary for them to play alongside their "social inferiors" if they were to win their bets. In time, a perception took hold that the typical amateur who played in first-class cricket, until 1962 when amateurism was abolished, was someone with a public school education who had then gone to one of Cambridge or Oxford University – society insisted that such people were "officers and gentlemen" whose destiny was to provide leadership. In a purely financial sense, the cricketing amateur would theoretically claim expenses for playing while his professional counterpart played under contract and was paid a wage or match fee; in practice, many amateurs claimed more than actual expenditure and the derisive term "shamateur" was coined to describe the practice.

- The Young Cricketer, 1768

The game underwent major development in the 18th century to become England's national sport.Its success was underwritten by the twin necessities of patronage and betting. Cricket was prominent in London as early as 1707 and, in the middle years of the century, large crowds flocked to matches on the Artillery Ground in Finsbury. The single wicket form of the sport attracted huge crowds and wagers to match, its popularity peaking in the 1748 season. Bowling underwent an evolution around 1760 when bowlers began to pitch the ball instead of rolling or skimming it towards the batter. This caused a revolution in bat design because, to deal with the bouncing ball, it was necessary to introduce the modern straight bat in place of the old "hockey stick" shape.

The Hambledon Club was founded in the 1760s and, for the next twenty years until the formation of Marylebone Cricket Club (MCC) and the opening of Lord's Old Ground in 1787, Hambledon was both the game's greatest club and its focal point. MCC quickly became the sport's premier club and the custodian of the Laws of Cricket. New Laws introduced in the latter part of the 18th century included the three stump wicket and leg before wicket (lbw).

The 19th century saw underarm bowling superseded by first roundarm and then overarm bowling. Both developments were controversial.Organisation of the game at county level led to the creation of the county clubs, starting with Sussex in 1839. In December 1889, the eight leading county clubs formed the official County Championship, which began in 1890.

The most famous player of the 19th century was W. G. Grace, who started his long and influential career in 1865. It was especially during the career of Grace that the distinction between amateurs and professionals became blurred by the existence of players like him who were nominally amateur but, in terms of their financial gain, de facto professional. Grace himself was said to have been paid more money for playing cricket than any professional.

The last two decades before the First World War have been called the "Golden Age of cricket". It is a nostalgic name prompted by the collective sense of loss resulting from the war, but the period did produce some great players and memorable matches, especially as organised competition at county and Test level developed.

- Cricket becomes an international sport

In 1844, the first-ever international match took place between the United States and Canada. In 1859, a team of English players went to North America on the first overseas tour. Meanwhile, the British Empire had been instrumental in spreading the game overseas and by the middle of the 19th century it had become well established in Australia, the Caribbean, India, Pakistan, New Zealand, North America and South Africa.

In 1862, an English team made the first tour of Australia. The first Australian team to travel overseas consisted of Aboriginal stockmen who toured England in 1868. The first One Day International match was played on 5 January 1971 between Australia and England at the Melbourne Cricket Ground.

In 1876–77, an England team took part in what was retrospectively recognised as the first-ever Test match at the Melbourne Cricket Ground against Australia. The rivalry between England and Australia gave birth to The Ashes in 1882, and this has remained Test cricket's most famous contest. Test cricket began to expand in 1888–89 when South Africa played England.

- World cricket in the 20th century

The inter-war years were dominated by Australia's Don Bradman, statistically the greatest Test batter of all time. Test cricket continued to expand during the 20th century with the addition of the West Indies (1928),

New Zealand (1930) and India (1932) before the Second World War and then Pakistan (1952), Sri Lanka (1982), Zimbabwe (1992), Bangladesh (2000), Ireland and Afghanistan (both 2018) in the post-war period. South Africa was banned from international cricket from 1970 to 1992 as part of the apartheid boycott.

- The rise of limited overs cricket

Cricket entered a new era in 1963 when English counties introduced the limited overs variant. As it was sure to produce a result, limited overs cricket was lucrative and the number of matches increased. The first Limited Overs International was played in 1971 and the governing International Cricket Council (ICC), seeing its potential, staged the first limited overs Cricket World Cup in 1975. In the 21st century, a new limited overs form, Twenty20, made an immediate impact. On 22 June 2017, Afghanistan and Ireland became the 11th and 12th ICC full members, enabling them to play Test cricket.

- A typical cricket field.

In cricket, the rules of the game are specified in a code called The Laws of Cricket (hereinafter called "the Laws") which has a global remit. There are 42 Laws (always written with a capital "L"). The earliest known version of the code was drafted in 1744 and, since 1788, it has been owned and maintained by its custodian, the Marylebone Cricket Club (MCC) in London.

- Playing area

Cricket is a bat-and-ball game played on a cricket field between two teams of eleven players each. The field is usually circular or oval in shape and the edge of the playing area is marked by a boundary, which may be a fence, part of the stands, a rope, a painted line or a combination of these; the boundary must if possible be marked along its entire length.

In the approximate centre of the field is a rectangular pitch (see image, below) on which a wooden target called a wicket is sited at each end; the wickets are placed 22 yards (20 m) apart. The pitch is a flat surface 10 feet (3.0 m) wide, with very short grass that tends to be worn away as the game progresses (cricket can also be played on artificial surfaces, notably matting). Each wicket is made of three wooden stumps topped by two bails.

- Cricket pitch and creases

As illustrated above, the pitch is marked at each end with four white painted lines: a bowling crease, a popping crease and two return creases. The three stumps are aligned centrally on the bowling crease, which is eight feet eight inches long. The popping crease is drawn four feet in front of the bowling crease and parallel to it; although it is drawn as a twelve-foot line (six feet either side of the wicket), it is, in fact, unlimited in length. The return creases are drawn at right angles to the popping crease so that they intersect the ends of the bowling crease; each return crease is drawn as an eight-foot line, so that it extends four feet behind the bowling crease, but is also, in fact, unlimited in length.

Before a match begins, the team captains (who are also players) toss a coin to decide which team will bat first and so take the first innings. Innings is the term used for each phase of play in the match.In each innings, one team bats, attempting to score runs, while the other team bowls and fields the ball, attempting to restrict the scoring and dismiss the batters. When the first innings ends, the teams change roles; there can be two to four innings depending upon the type of match. A match with four scheduled innings is played over three to five days; a match with two scheduled innings is usually completed in a single day. During an innings, all eleven members of the fielding team take the field, but usually only two members of the batting team are on the field at any given time. The exception to this is if a batter has any type of illness or injury restricting his or her ability to run, in this case the batter is allowed a runner who can run between the wickets when the batter hits a scoring run or runs,though this does not apply in international cricket. The order of batters is usually announced just before the match, but it can be varied.

The main objective of each team is to score more runs than their opponents but, in some forms of cricket, it is also necessary to dismiss all of the opposition batters in their final innings in order to win the match, which would otherwise be drawn. If the team batting last is all out having scored fewer runs than their opponents, they are said to have "lost by n runs" (where n is the difference between the aggregate number of runs scored by the teams). If the team that bats last scores enough runs to win, it is said to have "won by n wickets", where n is the number of wickets left to fall. For example, a team that passes its opponents' total having lost six wickets (i.e., six of their batters have been dismissed) have won the match "by four wickets".

In a two-innings-a-side match, one team's combined first and second innings total may be less than the other side's first innings total. The team with the greater score is then said to have "won by an innings and n runs", and does not need to bat again: n is the difference between the two teams' aggregate scores. If the team batting last is all out, and both sides have scored the same number of runs, then the match is a tie; this result is quite rare in matches of two innings a side with only 62 happening in first-class matches from the earliest known instance in 1741 until January 2017. In the traditional form of the game, if the time allotted for the match expires before either side can win, then the game is declared a draw.

If the match has only a single innings per side, then a maximum number of overs applies to each innings. Such a match is called a "limited overs" or "one-day" match, and the side scoring more runs wins regardless of the number of wickets lost, so that a draw cannot occur. In some cases, ties are broken by having each team bat for a one-over innings known as a Super Over; subsequent Super Overs may be played if the first Super Over ends in a tie. If this kind of match is temporarily interrupted by bad weather, then a complex mathematical formula, known as the Duckworth–Lewis–Stern method after its developers, is often used to recalculate a new target score. A one-day match can also be declared a "no-result" if fewer than a previously agreed number of overs have been bowled by either team, in circumstances that make normal resumption of play impossible; for example, wet weather.

In all forms of cricket, the umpires can abandon the match if bad light or rain makes it impossible to continue. There have been instances of entire matches, even Test matches scheduled to be played over five days, being lost to bad weather without a ball being bowled: for example, the third Test of the 1970/71 series in Australia.

- Innings

The innings (ending with 's' in both singular and plural form) is the term used for each phase of play during a match. Depending on the type of match being played, each team has either one or two innings. Sometimes all eleven members of the batting side take a turn to bat but, for various reasons, an innings can end before they have all done so. The innings terminates if the batting team is "all out", a term defined by the Laws: "at the fall of a wicket or the retirement of a batter, further balls remain to be bowled but no further batter is available to come in". In this situation, one of the batters has not been dismissed and is termed not out; this is because he has no partners left and there must always be two active batters while the innings is in progress.

- An innings may end early while there are still two not out batters

the batting team's captain may declare the innings closed even though some of his players have not had a turn to bat: this is a tactical decision by the captain, usually because he believes his team have scored sufficient runs and need time to dismiss the opposition in their innings

the set number of overs (i.e., in a limited overs match) have been bowled

the match has ended prematurely due to bad weather or running out of time

in the final innings of the match, the batting side has reached its target and won the game.

- Overs

The Laws state that, throughout an innings, "the ball shall be bowled from each end alternately in overs of 6 balls". The name "over" came about because the umpire calls "Over!" when six balls have been bowled. At this point, another bowler is deployed at the other end, and the fielding side changes ends while the batters do not. A bowler cannot bowl two succcssive overs, although a bowler can (and usually does) bowl alternate overs, from the same end, for several overs which are termed a "spell". The batters do not change ends at the end of the over, and so the one who was non-striker is now the striker and vice versa. The umpires also change positions so that the one who was at "square leg" now stands behind the wicket at the non-striker's end and vice versa.

- Clothing and equipment

English cricketer W. G. Grace "taking guard" in 1883. His pads and bat are very similar to those used today. The gloves have evolved somewhat. Many modern players use more defensive equipment than were available to Grace, most notably helmets and arm guards.

The wicket-keeper (a specialised fielder behind the batter) and the batters wear protective gear because of the hardness of the ball, which can be delivered at speeds of more than 145 kilometres per hour (90 mph) and presents a major health and safety concern. Protective clothing includes pads (designed to protect the knees and shins), batting gloves or wicket-keeper's gloves for the hands, a safety helmet for the head and a box for male players inside the trousers (to protect the crotch area). Some batters wear additional padding inside their shirts and trousers such as thigh pads, arm pads, rib protectors and shoulder pads. The only fielders allowed to wear protective gear are those in positions very close to the batter (i.e., if they are alongside or in front of him), but they cannot wear gloves or external leg guards.

Subject to certain variations, on-field clothing generally includes a collared shirt with short or long sleeves; long trousers; woolen pullover (if needed); cricket cap (for fielding) or a safety helmet; and spiked shoes or boots to increase traction. The kit is traditionally all white and this remains the case in Test and first-class cricket but, in limited overs cricket, team colours are worn instead.

- Bat and ball

Two types of cricket ball, both of the same size:

i) A used white ball. White balls are mainly used in limited overs cricket, especially in matches played at night, under floodlights (left).

ii) A used red ball. Red balls are used in Test cricket, first-class cricket and some other forms of cricket (right).

The essence of the sport is that a bowler delivers (i.e., bowls) the ball from his or her end of the pitch towards the batter who, armed with a bat, is "on strike" at the other end (see next sub-section: Basic gameplay).

The bat is made of wood, usually Salix alba (white willow), and has the shape of a blade topped by a cylindrical handle. The blade must not be more than 4.25 inches (10.8 cm) wide and the total length of the bat not more than 38 inches (97 cm). There is no standard for the weight, which is usually between 2 lb 7 oz and 3 lb (1.1 and 1.4 kg).

The ball is a hard leather-seamed spheroid, with a circumference of 9 inches (23 cm). The ball has a "seam": six rows of stitches attaching the leather shell of the ball to the string and cork interior. The seam on a new ball is prominent and helps the bowler propel it in a less predictable manner. During matches, the quality of the ball deteriorates to a point where it is no longer usable; during the course of this deterioration, its behaviour in flight will change and can influence the outcome of the match. Players will, therefore, attempt to modify the ball's behaviour by modifying its physical properties. Polishing the ball and wetting it with sweat or saliva is legal, even when the polishing is deliberately done on one side only to increase the ball's swing through the air, but the acts of rubbing other substances into the ball, scratching the surface or picking at the seam are illegal ball tampering.

- Player roles

Basic gameplay: bowler to batter

During normal play, thirteen players and two umpires are on the field. Two of the players are batters and the rest are all eleven members of the fielding team. The other nine players in the batting team are off the field in the pavilion. The image with overlay below shows what is happening when a ball is being bowled and which of the personnel are on or close to the pitch.

- Return crease

In the photo, the two batters (3 & 8; wearing yellow) have taken position at each end of the pitch (6). Three members of the fielding team (4, 10 & 11; wearing dark blue) are in shot. One of the two umpires (1; wearing white hat) is stationed behind the wicket (2) at the bowler's (4) end of the pitch. The bowler (4) is bowling the ball (5) from his end of the pitch to the batter at the other end who is called the "striker". The other batter (3) at the bowling end is called the "non-striker". The wicket-keeper (10), who is a specialist, is positioned behind the striker's wicket (9) and behind him stands one of the fielders in a position called "first slip" (11). While the bowler and the first slip are wearing conventional kit only, the two batters and the wicket-keeper are wearing protective gear including safety helmets, padded gloves and leg guards (pads).

While the umpire (1) in shot stands at the bowler's end of the pitch, his colleague stands in the outfield, usually in or near the fielding position called "square leg", so that he is in line with the popping crease (7) at the striker's end of the pitch. The bowling crease (not numbered) is the one on which the wicket is located between the return creases (12). The bowler (4) intends to hit the wicket (9) with the ball (5) or, at least, to prevent the striker (8) from scoring runs. The striker (8) intends, by using his bat, to defend his wicket and, if possible, to hit the ball away from the pitch in order to score runs.

Some players are skilled in both batting and bowling, or as either or these as well as wicket-keeping, so are termed all-rounders. Bowlers are classified according to their style, generally as fast bowlers, seam bowlers or spinners. Batters are classified according to whether they are right-handed or left-handed.

- Fielding

Of the eleven fielders, three are in shot in the image above. The other eight are elsewhere on the field, their positions determined on a tactical basis by the captain or the bowler. Fielders often change position between deliveries, again as directed by the captain or bowler.

If a fielder is injured or becomes ill during a match, a substitute is allowed to field instead of him, but the substitute cannot bowl or act as a captain, except in the case of concussion substitutes in international cricket. The substitute leaves the field when the injured player is fit to return. The Laws of Cricket were updated in 2017 to allow substitutes to act as wicket-keepers.

- Bowling and dismissal

Glenn McGrath of Australia holds the world record for most wickets in the Cricket World Cup.

Most bowlers are considered specialists in that they are selected for the team because of their skill as a bowler, although some are all-rounders and even specialist batters bowl occasionally. The specialists bowl several times during an innings but may not bowl two overs consecutively. If the captain wants a bowler to "change ends", another bowler must temporarily fill in so that the change is not immediate.

A bowler reaches his delivery stride by means of a "run-up" and an over is deemed to have begun when the bowler starts his run-up for the first delivery of that over, the ball then being "in play".

Fast bowlers, needing momentum, take a lengthy run up while bowlers with a slow delivery take no more than a couple of steps before bowling. The fastest bowlers can deliver the ball at a speed of over 145 kilometres per hour (90 mph) and they sometimes rely on sheer speed to try to defeat the batter, who is forced to react very quickly.

Other fast bowlers rely on a mixture of speed and guile by making the ball seam or swing (i.e. curve) in flight. This type of delivery can deceive a batter into miscuing his shot, for example, so that the ball just touches the edge of the bat and can then be "caught behind" by the wicket-keeper or a slip fielder. At the other end of the bowling scale is the spin bowler who bowls at a relatively slow pace and relies entirely on guile to deceive the batter. A spinner will often "buy his wicket" by "tossing one up" (in a slower, steeper parabolic path) to lure the batter into making a poor shot. The batter has to be very wary of such deliveries as they are often "flighted" or spun so that the ball will not behave quite as he expects and he could be "trapped" into getting himself out. In between the pacemen and the spinners are the medium paced seamers who rely on persistent accuracy to try to contain the rate of scoring and wear down the batter's concentration.

There are nine ways in which a batter can be dismissed: five relatively common and four extremely rare. The common forms of dismissal are bowled, caught, leg before wicket (lbw), run out and stumped. Rare methods are hit wicket,hit the ball twice, obstructing the field and timed out. The Laws state that the fielding team, usually the bowler in practice, must appeal for a dismissal before the umpire can give his decision. If the batter is out, the umpire raises a forefinger and says "Out!"; otherwise, he will shake his head and say "Not out".There is, effectively, a tenth method of dismissal, retired out, which is not an on-field dismissal as such but rather a retrospective one for which no fielder is credited.

- Batting, runs and extras

The directions in which a right-handed batter, facing down the page, intends to send the ball when playing various cricketing shots. The diagram for a left-handed batter is a mirror image of this one.

Batters take turns to bat via a batting order which is decided beforehand by the team captain and presented to the umpires, though the order remains flexible when the captain officially nominates the team. Substitute batters are generally not allowed, except in the case of concussion substitutes in international cricket.

In order to begin batting the batter first adopts a batting stance. Standardly, this involves adopting a slight crouch with the feet pointing across the front of the wicket, looking in the direction of the bowler, and holding the bat so it passes over the feet and so its tip can rest on the ground near to the toes of the back foot.

A skilled batter can use a wide array of "shots" or "strokes" in both defensive and attacking mode. The idea is to hit the ball to the best effect with the flat surface of the bat's blade. If the ball touches the side of the bat it is called an "edge". The batter does not have to play a shot and can allow the ball to go through to the wicketkeeper. Equally, he does not have to attempt a run when he hits the ball with his bat. Batters do not always seek to hit the ball as hard as possible, and a good player can score runs just by making a deft stroke with a turn of the wrists or by simply "blocking" the ball but directing it away from fielders so that he has time to take a run. A wide variety of shots are played, the batter's repertoire including strokes named according to the style of swing and the direction aimed: e.g., "cut", "drive", "hook", "pull".

The batter on strike (i.e. the "striker") must prevent the ball hitting the wicket, and try to score runs by hitting the ball with his bat so that he and his partner have time to run from one end of the pitch to the other before the fielding side can return the ball. To register a run, both runners must touch the ground behind the popping crease with either their bats or their bodies (the batters carry their bats as they run). Each completed run increments the score of both the team and the striker.

- Sachin Tendulkar is the only player to have scored one hundred international centuries

The decision to attempt a run is ideally made by the batter who has the better view of the ball's progress, and this is communicated by calling: usually "yes", "no" or "wait". More than one run can be scored from a single hit: hits worth one to three runs are common, but the size of the field is such that it is usually difficult to run four or more. To compensate for this, hits that reach the boundary of the field are automatically awarded four runs if the ball touches the ground en route to the boundary or six runs if the ball clears the boundary without touching the ground within the boundary. In these cases the batters do not need to run. Hits for five are unusual and generally rely on the help of "overthrows" by a fielder returning the ball. If an odd number of runs is scored by the striker, the two batters have changed ends, and the one who was non-striker is now the striker. Only the striker can score individual runs, but all runs are added to the team's total.

Additional runs can be gained by the batting team as extras (called "sundries" in Australia) due to errors made by the fielding side. This is achieved in four ways: no-ball, a penalty of one extra conceded by the bowler if he breaks the rules; wide, a penalty of one extra conceded by the bowler if he bowls so that the ball is out of the batter's reach bye, an extra awarded if the batter misses the ball and it goes past the wicket-keeper and gives the batters time to run in the conventional way leg bye, as for a bye except that the ball has hit the batter's body, though not his bat. If the bowler has conceded a no-ball or a wide, his team incurs an additional penalty because that ball (i.e., delivery) has to be bowled again and hence the batting side has the opportunity to score more runs from this extra ball.

- Specialist roles

Captain (cricket) and Wicket-keeper

The captain is often the most experienced player in the team, certainly the most tactically astute, and can possess any of the main skillsets as a batter, a bowler or a wicket-keeper. Within the Laws, the captain has certain responsibilities in terms of nominating his players to the umpires before the match and ensuring that his players conduct themselves "within the spirit and traditions of the game as well as within the Laws".

The wicket-keeper (sometimes called simply the "keeper") is a specialist fielder subject to various rules within the Laws about his equipment and demeanour. He is the only member of the fielding side who can effect a stumping and is the only one permitted to wear gloves and external leg guards. Depending on their primary skills, the other ten players in the team tend to be classified as specialist batters or specialist bowlers. Generally, a team will include five or six specialist batters and four or five specialist bowlers, plus the wicket-keeper.

- Umpires and scorers

Umpire (cricket), Scoring (cricket), and Cricket statistics

An umpire signals a decision to the scorers

The game on the field is regulated by the two umpires, one of whom stands behind the wicket at the bowler's end, the other in a position called "square leg" which is about 15–20 metres away from the batter on strike and in line with the popping crease on which he is taking guard. The umpires have several responsibilities including adjudication on whether a ball has been correctly bowled (i.e., not a no-ball or a wide); when a run is scored; whether a batter is out (the fielding side must first appeal to the umpire, usually with the phrase "How's that?" or "Owzat?"); when intervals start and end; and the suitability of the pitch, field and weather for playing the game. The umpires are authorised to interrupt or even abandon a match due to circumstances likely to endanger the players, such as a damp pitch or deterioration of the light.

Off the field in televised matches, there is usually a third umpire who can make decisions on certain incidents with the aid of video evidence. The third umpire is mandatory under the playing conditions for Test and Limited Overs International matches played between two ICC full member countries. These matches also have a match referee whose job is to ensure that play is within the Laws and the spirit of the game.

The match details, including runs and dismissals, are recorded by two official scorers, one representing each team. The scorers are directed by the hand signals of an umpire . For example, the umpire raises a forefinger to signal that the batter is out (has been dismissed); he raises both arms above his head if the batter has hit the ball for six runs. The scorers are required by the Laws to record all runs scored, wickets taken and overs bowled; in practice, they also note significant amounts of additional data relating to the game.

A match's statistics are summarised on a scorecard. Prior to the popularisation of scorecards, most scoring was done by men sitting on vantage points cuttings notches on tally sticks and runs were originally called notches.According to Rowland Bowen, the earliest known scorecard templates were introduced in 1776 by T. Pratt of Sevenoaks and soon came into general use.It is believed that scorecards were printed and sold at Lord's for the first time in 1846.

- thank you for buy & read this book

  have a great day of your
  from : Mr Vivek Kumar Pandey

- This All Credit Goes To My Super Hero Daddy. “Always Love You dad’.

Printed by Libri Plureos GmbH in Hamburg,
Germany